How to Fix Your Funnel

Maximizing Business Profit with Infusionsoft's Automation Software

by Ryan J Chapman

1st Edition 2013

Copyright © 2013 by Market Genius, LLC.

Published by Market Genius, LLC.

145 Vallecitos De Oro, Ste 203, San Marcos, CA 92069

Ryan Chapman

145 Vallecitos De Oro, Suite 203, San Marcos, CA, 92069

Printed in the United States of America

I couldn't have pulled together this work without the assistance of my family and team.

I'd like to thank them for their great patience and support as we pursue our mission to explode profits for small businesses across the world.

I'd also like to dedicate this work to the entrepreneur, where ever they may call home, who experiences all the emotions of owning a business.

May growing a business be a spiritual experience that brings all the richness of life to you and those you care for.

The world wouldn't be as good as it is without your countless hours, blood, sweat and tears.

About the Author

Ryan J Chapman

Ryan originally set his sights on being a dentist.

3 years into his pre-dental studies the entrepreneurial genes that are deeply embedded into his DNA wouldn't allow him to stay in school.

Ryan in this business attire. Suits are for monkeys.

After a number of failed business attempts, each adding another piece to the success puzzle, he finally found the last two pieces, direct response marketing and automation software (Infusionsoft), and success could not be held back any longer.

Together with his brother Trent, Ryan used Infusionsoft to take a training company from 0 to $1.3 Million in 12 months. What made this particularly exciting is they did it with 4 employees.

Over the years that followed Ryan trained hundreds of business owners on marketing, utilizing advanced technology to extend marketing and business automation and making business decisions based on a simple method described in this book.

Today Ryan principally works with private clients as he directs a software company (FixYourFunnel.com) that extends Infusionsoft's default marketing channels, a training company focused on small business owners and a consulting firm that designs and implements advanced marketing and business automation processes with Infusionsoft as a core technology.

While Ryan may not be contacted directly, requests to have an appointment to speak with Ryan can be sought by calling his office (760) 621-8199.

Ryan is a Southern California native, born and raised in San Marcos, California where he lives with is gorgeous wife and 6 wonderful children.

At the time of this publishing Ryan is the tallest of his 12 siblings at 6 foot 7 inches and dominates inside the key during family basketball games (*some of his more athletic brothers may argue this point, but they were not invited to comment by the editor*).

TABLE OF CONTENTS

Preface

WHO THIS BOOK IS FOR

Before I tell you who this book is really for, I'd like to tell you who it's not for.

If you are not in business to see how big you can grow your business, this book isn't for you.

If you're just looking to be comfortable with your business or comfortable with your lifestyle, then this book also isn't for you.

If you just want to be secure, this book isn't for you.

If you're satisfied with your income, free time or your anticipated future, then this book is not for you.

This book has been written specifically for those individuals, those business owners, those entrepreneurs, who really want to get the most out of their business.

Why do I even start this book with this discussion?

I recently had a call with a private client who indicated as I started to talk about profit growth, that he wasn't interested in profit growth. His business was 20 years old, it was very established and he just wanted to get some automation in place.

I told him that, *"We may not be a good fit if that's all you're looking for because what I do is I help people unlock hidden profits so we can increase overall profit flow, which means growth."*

And he mistook growth to be something that only happens with new companies...start ups.

The reality is is, if you make decisive choices and strategic decisions about your business versus only responding to whatever the market tells you, you can create a business that maintains continual growth and not just growth in terms of size or number of employees because that's really not the measure of success for a business, but growth in profit.

Understand that real profit, which is money you get to keep, is created because your business created real value for the marketplace. When a business creates profit growth, what it's really done is created more value for the marketplace and harvested that value effectively.

If that is not what you are about. If you're not interested in having a business that creates more and more value to the market place, then please give this book to someone who is.

This world is in desperate need of business owners who get it and will create more with what they have at their disposal.

Most of what you need to create continued profit growth is within your reach right now. It may be hidden to you, but it is within your reach.

In fact, most of what you need to know is already in your mind, but is simply lacking a structure to organize it in such a way that you can express your true business genius.

If you're interested in profit growth; not just revenue growth, not just number of employees growth, not just size of the facilities growth, not just expense growth, but profit growth, then **you're reading the right book**.

This book will begin with a little parable. It's not set in old England, or even the Arabian peninsula...it's set in Texas.

It would be very easy to skip. After all, your time is precious, you can't afford to be reading fiction, right? But this parable, like most parables holds a secret. A secret that sets the tone for the rest of the book. A secret to unlocking sustainable profit growth...so read it carefully.

Forward

THE GOAL OF A BUSINESS OWNER

By Trent Chapman

It was a hard question for me to answer...

"What do you want from your business?"

This question was posed to me years ago during a training I attended, back when I first started my real estate business.

I guess the answer we all initially come up with when we are asked why we started our business is *"more money"*, which means, more net profit.

Of course in our society we grow up learning that there is increased reward for those that take the risk of taking an idea for a business and making it a reality. Starting and running a business (*if done _right_*) should bring us more money.

However, once I really thought about it, what I REALLY wanted was more time to enjoy doing what I love with who I love.

I love traveling and experiencing new places and new foods.

I love my wife and children.

For me then it was clear that I wanted to travel and experience different parts of this wonderful World with my family.

That is my HUGE motivator. That is what I want from my business.

Freedom to travel and enough money to do it well.

Unfortunately, I am not the sharpest tool in the shed, so it took me a few years to really ask myself the question that should have followed right after I realized what I really wanted from my business.

I finally brought myself to ask, "*HOW can my business give me more free time and more money so I can really enjoy traveling with my wife and kids?*"

Once I had that clarity... that LIFESTYLE is what I wanted from my business and that I needed to PLAN on my business providing that lifestyle for me, it became more obvious WHERE I needed to spend time working ON my business and that I needed to make major adjustments to my business if I really wanted my business to provide me with freedom to travel with my family.

At the time, I was the sole cog running everything.

I didn't use leverage very well and I didn't grow at a rapid pace. I was comfortable, made good money, but was stuck in the business and couldn't travel.

I wasn't looking for a job or a place to hang out while I wasn't at home, but that's what my business had become.

A place to go from 8am-6pm whether I needed to be there or not.

Sure, I was making good money, but I wasn't really *"working"* the entire time. I was spending about half my time doing stuff I didn't need to do. Things that others could have done simply because I didn't have a PLAN to get what I wanted from my business.

I wanted the lifestyle owning a business could provide and if my business was not providing that, or worse, taking that lifestyle away from me, then I had to figure a way to change that or create another business that would realistically give me what I was after.

Although my motivation is clear to me, here are some of the top things I hear from other business owners about what THEY WANT from their businesses:

★ More net profit
★ Freedom to choose what they do with their time
★ Recognition

When I got into business for myself I guarantee you that for me, it was not for recognition, but it was because I had a strong belief that the value I could create would bring me profit which I could then exchange for:

1. Increased income and wealth which would provide a sense of financial security along with more of the nice things I wanted for me and my family or

2. More time to spend with my family while having all my personal needs taken care of.

It's obvious that more net profit is what every business owner wants from their business, because more net profit equates to more freedom.

Freedom to choose to use profit for more leverage by wisely increasing your marketing budget, wisely hiring effective people or improving systems through new technologies and systems to make more profit and build wealth.

It gives freedom to trade some of that net profit to hire someone to replace more of your daily functions in the business to have more free time to do what you want, ultimately, to have the lifestyle you choose to have come from your business.

Back to where we started.

All business owners want more net profit because that is the easiest thing to quantify and it can be traded for lifestyle in a very real way.

Besides more time or more wealth, some business owners have mentioned that recognition is the motivation for WHY they started their business and why they keep growing it.

Recognition from their peers, their in-laws, their friends and from the community for the good, for the time and sacrifice, for the value/benefit their business brings to market.

I almost left this next section about recognition out.

Most business owners will say they don't care for recognition, but they will gladly accept it when given.

We want the lifestyle a business can produce and the options and freedom that come with it.

We don't need recognition, but we gladly accept it when we receive it for the good we do for our local economies and the opportunities we provide for families in our community.

We all started out as just one man or one woman with an idea. You may be there right now yourself as you read this. The point is, it feels good to be acknowledged for all the time, effort, thought, persistence and risk that goes into building your business.

Recently a politician that shall remain nameless said something to the affect, "*...you didn't build your business on your own, other people made it possible... you aren't any smarter, you just had an opportunity to build your business because of other people.*"

While I don't know that those were the true intention of his words, it was taken that way by many business owners who became outraged.

Did those words affect the profitability of those businesses? Not at all. Why did they get upset?

One word...

Recognition.

We all have this desire to be acknowledged for all the sacrifice, sleepless nights, hard decisions, personal time away from family, skipped vacations, etc to BUILD a business so one day we could enjoy a more comfortable lifestyle.

It's personal and painful when someone tries to take away that sacrifice by making it sound like you did not build your business.

I am the first to admit that without good people on my team and without the opportunities that our free country has given me, I would not have near the level of success I enjoy. However... I still like to be recognized for the efforts I have put into starting and building my business.

Once you have a more comfortable lifestyle, you never forget what you went through to get there... so when people say things like, *"you didn't build that"*...it hurts.

As you continue to read this book, you'll notice that it is not written to help you get more recognition... but it will come as a by-product, at least from other business owners like us, who understand what you've gone through and what it takes to get to *"the sweet spot"* in your business where you can have the lifestyle you built your business to provide.

Ultimately we all want peace of mind, security, etc, but I've never felt so secure as when my income was in my hands, not a company who employed me and not in the hands of the government.

The clear objective of this book is to help you to be able to continuously unlock profit trapped in your business to feel more peace of mind and enjoy more net profit, whether you turn that into more free time, more wealth or both.

Chapter 1

THE PARABLE OF
THE PIPES

Bill was a proud Texan. He had been born and raised on the Texas flat lands and had picked up a nice parcel of land. He was enterprising and hard working.

One day his neighbor Walter approached him.

"Bill, as you know I have a rather large lake on my property. I aim to reduce the size of it considerably to remove a large swamp at the far end of it. If you're in the market for some water I'd be glad to let you take some off my hands for a penny a gallon."

Bill took this into consideration, but had no need for much lake water.

As fate would have it, the next day Bill's neighbor from the south, Howard, mentioned that he was looking for a mess of water and in a hurry.

"Bill, would you do me a favor? I'm looking to create a lake on my property and I mean a Texas size lake. If you hear of anyone with excess water I'd be more than happy to pay 5 cents a gallon to take it offer their hands."

Again, being enterprising Bill looked around his property and noticed an assortment of pipes of various diameters in one of his barns. In another barn he found a water pump he hadn't used in years but that would meet his needs nicely.

He approached both of his neighbors and struck a deal and began to arrange the pipes to span his property and began to move water. It was hard work, but soon water was flowing.

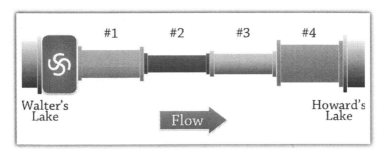

After a while Bill realized that he wasn't making as much money as he would like.

Bill removed his wide brimmed hat and wiped the sweat off his brow. *"What's keeping me from making more profit?"*

Then it hit him like a flash flood in September, *"I need bigger pipe!"*

Bill went to pipe 2 and swapped it out with a larger diameter pipe. Immediately profits increased! Bill was very impressed with himself, as he ought to have been. He had increased the profitability of his business!

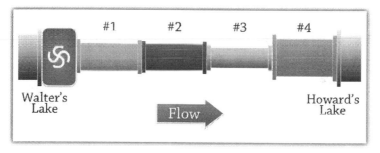

But it only took a day and Bill thought to himself, *"Why stop here? Walter ain't complaining about how much water I'm moving, why not take it up a notch?"*

Bill thought hard again. *"What do I need to do to increase profits even more???"*

Then he remembered what he had done the day before.

He quickly surveyed his barns and found a pipe that was even larger than the pipe he had swapped out the other day. He removed pipe 2 and upgraded it with an even larger pipe.

But when Bill went back to check out the progress he was puzzled at first, then flat out frustrated! Not only had profits not gone up, they'd actually gone down! His bill from Walter was higher and his income from Howard was the same as before the pipe was upgraded.

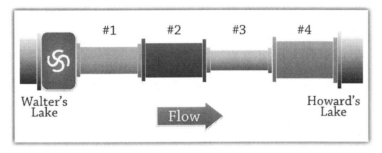

"*How is this possible??? Last time I replaced pipe 2 I saw an immediate bump in profits. Maybe I just need to turn up the pump. Push more water in and I'm sure to get more water out!*"

Bill turned up the pump, the pressure gauge swung into the red zone.

"Hum, that doesn't look good, but I won't keep it there for long, just long enough to see if that fixes the problem."

Bill took a stroll along the pipe to see how the increased pressure was effecting the pipes. He noticed water leaking out right after pipe 2. Pipe 3 looked like it was about to burst.

"That's it!" Bill shouted.

"I didn't need to make pipe 2 bigger, I needed to make pipe 3 bigger. It was the smallest diameter pipe in the mix after I upgraded pipe 2."

Bill was relieved that he had figured out why upgrading pipe 2 didn't increase profits, but has he rushed back to the pump to turn it down before pipe 3 busted, he wondered why his overhead had gone up.

Then he remembered science class. The volume of pipe 2 had gone up, but the flow had not because of the volume of pipe 3 had stayed the same!

Overhead had gone up because he had more water in pipe 2 now.

That was it!

Bill was suddenly much more excited than he had been the day he had upgraded pipe 2 for the first time. He not only had discovered how to increase profits, but how to constantly increase profits.

When Bill got back to the house for lunch he grabbed a piece of paper and wrote out some rules for determining how he could improve flow and as a result profit in his water moving enterprise.

Rule 1: Figure out which pipe is determining the overall flow of water. At some point it may be the pump, so don't rule that out either.

Rule 2: Don't do anything else until the pipe (or pump, as the case may be) has been upgraded to the point that it is no longer limiting the overall flow of water.

Rule 3: Go back to rule #1.

Bill was so pleased with his rules he determined to have Fred, the local sign painter, come over to the house and paint the rules on the South side of his biggest barn.

There was no way he'd forget these rules...ever.

Fred showed up the next day and got right to work. But as the story normally goes in small towns, Fred was dying to know why Bill was having him paint these rules on the side of his barn.

"Bill, I'm sorry, but I can't paint another letter until I know what these rules are all about."

"Fred, it's really quite simple. See, I'm helping Howard out by moving water from Walter's lake to his. Howard pays me a few cents per gallon and I pay Walter a penny a gallon. I keep the difference for my time and trouble."

"OK, but what's that got to do with them there rules?"

"Fred, come on now! Read 'em. As much as I like Howard and Walter, I ain't laying pipe and firing up the pump for fun. It's about profit. They got needs and I've got a solution. But I only get paid for how well I help them out. Well anyone knows that the faster I can move water the more money I'll make. These rules are about making more profit!"

"Well, Bill, we've known each other for a long time. And I've got to say, I could use more profit. Could I use these rules to make more profit? I mean, I'm not moving water, I'm painting signs."

"Hum...let me think about that Fred. I'm not quite sure off the top of my head how to make these rules work for you, since you ain't using pipe or nothing, but I'm sure they'd help you."

"Well, I don't have any pipe, or a pump in my business."

"Now Fred, I don't know that you got to have any pipe to make this work. I mean, my pipes are designed to move the water, for which I get paid the difference between my cost and what I can sell it for. What do you get paid for?"

"Why, painting signs of course. But it's not so simple as painting a sign. I need someone like you who needs a sign painted. That can be hard to know ahead of time."

"So your profit is determined by how many people want you to paint a sign for them, right?"

"Well, not exactly."

"How's that?"

"Well, it's one thing to have someone want me to paint the sign, but then I've got to check out where I'm painting the sign to see what kind of scaffolding I'll need, and hope I've got enough so I don't have to *break it down and move it part way through. Then I've got to figure out how much paint I'm going to need, how long it will take, and match that against the time frame of the customer. And I wish that where the end of it!"*

"Fred, that sounds like the end of it!"

"Nope. With someone like you, I know I'll be paid as soon as the job is done, but some folks like to drag their feet paying me so I end up chasing down my money, which I need to cover all my expenses."

"That's it then!"

"What do you mean Bill?"

"Your pipes are all the parts of your business that must be done in order before you get paid and see your profit."

"You have your marketing to get business. Your sales to close business. Your processes for getting everything out to the job and getting it done and then collecting payment."

"I've got 4 pipes!"

"I guess for you, we'd add a rule before my first rule. Your rule number 1 is to determine what dependent steps are necessary to create profit in your business."

"I guess I've only got to do that once…unless I change my business."

"Exactly!"

"OK, I'm going to write down my rules then and you let me know if I need to change anything."

Rule 1: Determine what dependent steps or processes are necessary to create a profit.

Rule 2: Figure out what my relative ability is to do each step.

Rule 3: Determine which step is limiting my profit.

Rule 4: Focus entirely on increasing my ability to do that step until it is no longer limiting my profit and let's my profit increase to the point that it stops increasing.

Rule 5: Go back to Rule 2.

"Fred, not only do I think you've got it, I think you're now the teacher!"

"Bill, I can't thank you enough. I'd like to paint your rules on the barn if you don't mind. I can see how these rules are going to change everything for me."

"Fred, I'll make you a deal. You make me a copy of your rules and finish up this wall today and I won't pay you."

Fred laughed and agreed!

Bill was excited for Fred, but when he saw the profit that month after applying his rules a few more times he was ecstatic!

A few months went by and Bill was in town checking out a new truck at the local dealership and who should he run into...Fred!

"Fred, you looking into a new truck? You've been driving old betsy there for years. Won't she be jealous?"

"Bill, I don't think you know how good a deal I got from you that day I painted your rules on your wall."

"What do you mean?"

"Well, I'm not buying a new truck to replace betsy. I did that a couple months back. This here truck is the 3rd in my new fleet. I've got 3 full time sign painters working for me all over the county now."

"What? You're pulling my leg!"

"No sir. I took those rules to heart and I've made it a regular practice to follow them religiously. I've never done so well. In fact, Bill, do you have plans for dinner this Friday? I'd love to take you out to that new steak house."

"Fred, I'd be honored. But only if you promise to fill me in on ALL the details."

Putting it to Work

What are the pipes of your business? Draw and label the pipes in your business in the space below.

Chapter 2

PROFIT IS THE MEASURE OF SUCCESS

People, when they talk about success, are all over the board.

Some people think of success as a relative term.

"Success is what you decide it is."

Others have a very concrete financial definition.

"Success is having 30 Million Dollars in gold in a safe in your basement."

And others would define it in terms of freedom. Regardless of how you define success as an individual, business success has a finite definition.

What do you think is the answer to the question of, *"What makes a business a success?"* Let's consider why businesses exist.

A business, by definition, is an entity that has been created for the purpose of generating profit.

A business has an ultimate measure of success and that ultimate measure of success is **profit**.

While it's common in today's public company arena to see companies who don't turn a profit for years, requiring heaving investment to maintain continued operations...

...and while some might consider those businesses to be a success, in terms of the actual ultimate measure of business success, they are currently a **failure**.

Will they some day be a success in terms of the ultimate measure of business success? Possibly. But, right now, they're a failure.

If you want to know if your business is a success, look at the profit.

Don't get me wrong.

There are other measures of success for other entities. If you're an organization, like a charity or a church, then the ultimate measure of success is not profit. It is something entirely different.

If you have an association or a community, the ultimate measure of success is not profit there either.

But, when we talk about a business, the whole point of the business is to make profit. If the business doesn't make profit, then we know it's not succeeding.

Is it OK to make a profit?

A common question people have internally, though they may not ever vocalize it, but it certainly does play a big part in the decisions they make as a business owner, is *"Is it OK to make a profit?"*

Capitalism has been demonized, especially more recently, with politicians claiming that if you make a certain amount of money, then the government's entitled to rob you of it.

But, the reality is, it is a good thing to make a profit.

A profit that is created by creating value for the customer is a very good thing, and without it the world wouldn't be nearly as nice as it is.

I'd go so far to say that a bulk of the world's issues would be resolved if only REAL profit were created in greater abundance.

SIDE NOTE: When I say REAL profit, I mean profit that is created from the creation of real value to the marketplace. Admittedly there are circumstances where a company or individual will extract money from the marketplace that was not the result of creating value, but from creating the illusion of value.

The difference between real value and the illusion of value is that the customer is not tricked into believing that what they bought was something entirely different from what they received.

While I give allowance to businesses who may have a small percentage of their customer base who simply are not that intelligent and may claim illusion, the business who has a majority of their customers up in arms over the illusion clearly has not created real profit and will inevitably be stripped of it, in terms of finances or freedom.

Creating REAL profit means you're increasing the convenience, and the quality of living of the customer. And whenever the customer ends up better off for having done business with your company, then you've done a good thing.

The more profit you can make by creating more value for the customer is something to be applauded and pursued.

If your business makes REAL profit, be happy about that, so long as you're creating real value for the customer.

The Ultimate Metric for Any Business...

What is the ultimate metric for business?

For many businesses, it will be a question of cash flow. In fact, cash flow is a critically important metric for business. Run out of cash and you're toast.

Shoot, when I put it that way it seems like cash flow IS the ultimate metric for any business!

But while cash flow may keep you around, it doesn't guarantee you're creating a profit, much less a profit worthy of your limited time on this Earth.

The true ULTIMATE metric that is the most important metric in any business is **profit flow**.

Paying attention to cash flow is essential to maintain the business, but to grow the business, the key is profit flow.

Interestingly enough if you choose to google "*profit flow*" you'll get 21,700 results at the time I searched.

Do the same thing for "*cash flow*" and you'll get 56.6 MILLION results. What does that tell you?

It tells me that the VAST majority of business owners are so focused on surviving that profit flow isn't even on their horizon. Is it any wonder that so few businesses will last?

> *Don't have a game plan that focuses on cash flow alone.*
>
> *Make sure that your game plan focuses on profit growth. Profit growth is a function of profit flow.*

The more profit you can create, flowing through your company, then the more you can experience profit growth.

Profit growth, then creates a company that grows not in terms of number of employees or revenue or number of locations, but in terms of meeting the measure of its creation.

Putting it to Work

Do you have a profit flow goal? Write down the profit flow multiple you want to create in the next 12 months. This a single number that represents how much profit flow will increase in the next year.

If your company currently generates X in profit, and you set the goal of 3 then your profit in 12 months would be 3X.

What's your number? _____

(Do you wonder what's realistic? Or have you vacillated because you have no idea how you'll accomplish the goal? If you promise to come back I'll give you permission to continue reading before you commit. Do you promise?)

Chapter 3

A BUSINESS IS A SYSTEM

When I use the word system, a lot of things could come to your mind.

You may be thinking of a system in terms of different processes that are put in place in order for you to accomplish something.

The dictionary definition that captures this is, "*An organized and coordinated method; a procedure.*"

This is probably the most common use of the word.

And to an extent that's an appropriate definition for system as it describes a business.

But, when I say system, I'm talking about it in the *scientific* sense.

In science, when we talk about a system, it is, "*A group of interacting, interrelated, or interdependent elements forming a complex whole.*"

And when we talk about a system, normally, we're talking about it in terms of physics. And, in physics, we're usually talking about the flow of energy.

If our system is a closed system then that tells us that energy can't escape, it can only change forms, and as a result the total energy in a system remains the same even though it may change form.

If we want to harness that energy then we need to be able to control the flow of it, and as we do we create power.

Well, let's take that same analogy and let's apply that to your business.

I want to think about it with you in the terms of the scientific meaning. Your business is a series of interdependent processes that end up with the result of creating a profit.

If those processes work properly, then a profit is generated.

If they are not working together properly, then, less profit or a loss will be created.

A system is a very interesting thing because, in science, we learn that a system that has a flow of energy can only have one limitation at any point in time. And, as you probably picked up from the parable of the pipes, a pipe is a really good metaphor for a business system.

The fact that your business is like a series of pipes should make you very EXCITED!

For me personally, the fact that my business can only have one thing that limits profit flow at any given time is very exciting.

I'm a relatively simple person.

I gravitate toward simple solutions. If you told me that there were 4 simultaneous things that limit the flow of profit in my business I'd be overwhelmed.

And, it would be nearly impossible for anyone to ever create profit growth if you had to work 4 things at the same time to create it.

But I know from personal experience that it is a fact that only one thing can control profit flow at a time. And because of this fact, you too should be psyched out of your gourd!

It means creating profit growth is very easy for you to be able to manage. You can create unlimited profit growth by being able to go through a cycle of determining what's limiting the flow of profit and then removing that limitation.

You've already be introduced to the method by which this is done in Chapter 1, but in subsequent chapters we're going to define the method in greater detail.

The secret to unlocking profit flow is finding that one thing that limits profit flow and reducing it, or eliminating it entirely.

If you want true profit growth, you're going to have to find that one thing that is limiting profit right now and reduce that limitation.

The debate over the existence of Silver Bullets.

One of the truths we hold on to quite well with our logical minds and seem to abandon recklessly when being sold is the idea that there is no such thing as a silver bullet.

A silver bullet is that one thing that will fix everything. The term originates out of the story of werewolves. No, not team Jacob, go back further.

Every villain has a weakness, otherwise a story is too depressing, or the villain ends up being the hero.

In werewolf lore, the only thing that can kill the werewolf is silver, and once the bullet was developed, then it became the perfect mechanism to deliver it.

Look at the havoc a werewolf creates! Maiming and killing the townsfolk! Who wouldn't want to get rid of that menace!

So the hero shows up, hunts down the source of all the mayhem and then takes aim and BAM! The thing that caused all the headaches and heartaches is gone.

Done.

Finito.

And thus the silver bullet legend was born and killed at the same time.

Born because the idea was introduced that there is a core problem that if hunted down and found could be eliminated with a single shot.

Killed because rationally thinking individuals would never consider that problems in a complex world...a real world, not a story book world, could be solved with a single, well placed shot.

It's the nature of most of our challenges in business. It's a problem of mis-association.

One of the most common methods for selling is to prop up the product or service as the end all be all, the "Silver Bullet".

The problem is that often it's more like a pewter bullet.

Well, I'll tell you what...the last thing I'd like to do is be facing a drooling, angry, long clawed, sharp fanged werewolf with nothing but a bunch of pewter bullets.

They say that pewter bullets don't even slow down werewolves. Serious.

Why Werewolves and Silver Bullets?

If most of what we think should be silver bullets end up being pewter bullets. It's no wonder that we don't believe that a Silver Bullet can exist.

It's no wonder that when we are presented with a simple method for getting to what we want, we hesitate and assume it's a trap or there is a gimmick or simply won't work!

There is a werewolf in your business. Fortunately it doesn't kill or maim people. Unfortunately it moves with ease, almost undetected.

It's what limits profit in your business right now. It's the pipe with the smallest diameter. It's the core limitation that prevents profit flow from growing.

Most of the business owners you know have no idea that they have their own werewolf. It's creating havoc in their companies. You now know.

What I'm presenting to you is a Silver Bullet. Because I've revealed this fact to you, I run great risk that you'll drop it on the ground, discounting it all.

But it's the fact that there is a silver bullet and that it can kill your werewolf that you can create a continually growing business that produces more and more profit.

The biggest limitation on business owners I've ever witnessed has always sat between their ears. It's true for me and it's true for you.

What will you choose to believe.

Could a Silver Bullet exist?

Putting it to Work

Watch the video on business growth. Use your mobile phone to read the QR Code to the below.

Chapter 4

WHEN TECHNOLOGY PRODUCES PROFIT

Technology *can* produce profit.

Perhaps, one of the most impactful people on my business philosophy has been Dr. Eliyahu Goldratt, who passed away in 2011.

Dr. Goldratt was a physicist who moved into the manufacturing industry and ended up having some impact into sales and marketing, while not as profound as his impact on manufacturing.

One of the most profound statements he ever made was on the subject of technology and potential benefits that could spring from it.

He said:

"Technology can bring benefits if, and only if, it reduces a limitation."

Read that sentence again, and read it carefully.

What we will do for the remainder of this book is built on this premise that technology has the capacity to create or bring benefits.

For our discussion I'm going to modify the quote slightly.

Technology can produce profit if, and only if, the technology reduces the limitation on the flow of profit.

It's a slight variation, but let's investigate this variation because, as we do, you're going to gain two incredible benefits.

1. Absolute clarity on what YOU need to focus on at any given point in time.

2. Total confidence in your decision making process.

Most Dangerous Thing an Entrepreneur Can Do...

One of the most dangerous things we face as entrepreneurs is the fact that we can only really focus in on one thing at a time.

We may have a number of projects that we start, but we can only really focus in on one thing at a time.

And the challenge that we have as entrepreneurs isn't really working hard enough. I've never met a true entrepreneur that was lazy. If there is any causation made against an entrepreneur it's that they are work-o-holics.

No, you don't need to worry about working hard. In fact you don't even need to worry about working smart. I can say that will all confidence because you're reading this book. The fact that you are reading any book is a testament to the fact that you strive to and do work smart.

It's working hard enough on the **right** things.

If you truly are an entrepreneur then I know that you've worked hard and smart in the wrong direction at least once in your life. So you know from your gut what I'm talking about. What vexes us most is wondering if the direction we're steering the boat is the **RIGHT** direction.

Once you are confident that you're headed in the right direction, look out, because you're going to reach your objectives.

What we don't have is the luxury of being wrong for very long.

Take Coca-cola. In the 80's they came out with NEW Coke. Think about the resources, time, effort, energy that went into creating the new formula, designing the new cans, pulling together the marketing campaign, making all the arrangements for the launch and then having it fall flat.

What would an investment in that direction do to your company? Would it just absorb it and continue on for decades unscathed?

The reality is we don't have the luxury to be wrong for long. You need certainty. Not 100%, but pretty close. It used to be that you couldn't get that close. Mostly because all your business decisions have a major factor called the "*Gut Factor*".

But, what is the right direction?

What is the first step?

What is the correct direction for us as entrepreneurs?

Well, it actually lies in the secret Dr. Goldratt shared and I modified, so let's get into it more deeply.

> *Technology **can** produce profit **if, and only if**, the technology **reduces the limitation** on the flow of profit.*

The first key word I want to point out to you there is **can**.

Can means there is the possibility that something will produce profit, but that there is also the possibility that it won't. It is uncertain, but possible.

Technology has the potential and possibility of being a direct factor in the production of increased profit flow.

It's critically important that you buy into the fact that it's merely a possibility not a guaranteed result. The source of many an entrepreneur's broken business is in the poor assumption that introducing a technology would create profit.

Had they only known what you do now, that technology only carries the possibility of producing profit, they could have avoided the heartache!

Let's look at the next part of our key phrase: **if, and only if**.

That is a very *declarative* statement.

It means there are no if's, ands or buts about it. The condition that follows if, and only if MUST exist for the possibility of technology producing profit.

The definitive nature of this clause is extremely empowering because it clears up any ambiguity about what conditions must exist to allow technology to even have the possibility of producing profit.

Now to fully grasp the full meaning of this key sentence, let's examine the condition on which it all hinges...**reduces THE limitation**...

The limitation on what? Profit flow.

In order for the technology to have the possibility to produce profit, it must reduce the limitation on the flow of profit.

What limits the flow of profit. The use of the word "*THE*" implies that there is only one. I refer to this limitation as the core limitation to distinguish from other limitations that may exist in the business but are not the limitation that controls the flow of profit.

If you're not the analytical type...

...I want to commend you for reading up until this point. If you just skipped to here because of the big type above, then I'm going to encourage you to stiffen your upper lip and read through the entire chapter.

I only ask this of you for one reason. The entire philosophy and the results it produces that this book is all about hinge on your agreement with the entire depth of meaning this simple sentence proposes.

The approach embedded in this one sentence is the key to unlocking hidden profits in your business with automation software like Infusionsoft.

Those who do not understand this one sentence end up bloodied and beaten on the side of the road that leads to profit growth.

They fight against the technology while they think they are controlling it. If they do find some success it's a fraction of what is possible and most likely purely accidental as it is inconsistent with the principles that lead to profit growth.

On the flip side, if you understand what this simple sentence holds, then you'll know that it doesn't matter if you increase other areas in your business in terms of their productivity or their ability to perform, if that area doesn't limit profit.

If the limitation we focus on doesn't limit profit and yet we increase it's capacity, it does nothing to increase the flow of profit in our businesses.

In fact, any time energy, effort, or resources we put into reducing that limitation that is not the core limitation will be completely wasted!

Until the technology reduces the core limitation, implementing it produces the opposite impact from what we wanted...it reduces the flow of profit in that system.

How is that possible? Remember what happened in the parable when the wrong pipe was replaced?

It's true in business, not just the parable.

If cash flow is really that critical to survival, then we can safely say that any cash spent on a limitation that doesn't control profit flow is not only wasted, but also carries the lost opportunity cost as well.

This means that not only does the business not increase profit, but the resources available to increase profit have been spent ineffectively.

Suppose you spend a lot of money on lead generation, but your ability to convert those leads is abysmal, it won't matter if you spend more and more money on lead generation.

You're not going to significantly convert capital invested into lead generation into profit until you address your ability to convert those leads into sales.

Any time you spend working on the delivery of the product or in getting more leads or even better leads is not going to improve the profit of the business as substantially, as it would if you just addressed your conversion process.

Time of Reflection

You may have read what I've written so far and thought to yourself, *"Well, that's not entirely true, Ryan. I've increased profits before by just pumping more leads into a system that didn't have great conversion ratio."*

And I won't contest that at all.

That's entirely true.

But, you didn't experience dramatic profit growth and *anybody* can create incremental profit growth. I'm surely not going to call my mom up and tell her I increased profit marginally and at the same time broke down our sales conversion process further because I didn't want to focus on what was really limiting profit.

But that's exactly what you did if you just threw more leads a poorly converting sales process.

In fact, I'm going to wager a guess that if any people were involved in the sales process your conversion went down instead of holding steady.

And your retention or referrals also dropped.

Why can I say that? I've seen it too many times to count. When you turn up the pump instead of addressing the core limitation, you don't create transformational and significant profit growth.

What you really want is dramatic profit growth and that's what focusing in on this one simple sentence can do for you.

Putting it to Work

Below is a QR Code that will load a text message on your smart phone. You may scan it or text VIDEO to (760) 621-8199 to receive 4 videos from a presentation I gave on how to find out what your pipes are and how to discover your limitation. When you text in you'll receive a link to the videos.

I gave this presentation in September 2012 to a small group of hand picked individuals in San Diego. I was told a few months later by one of them (during a private consultation) that the attendees had stayed in the parking lot talking about what I had taught them for well over an hour.

They said it was more valuable to them than any $3,000 training they had ever attended.

Don't take my word for it, you can be the judge...

Chapter 5

THE WRONG APPROACH TO AUTOMATION

The wrong approach is probably the most common way that people get into an automation software, like Infusionsoft.

They hear some stories of people who made big bucks using Infusionsoft or they see some features that directly correlate with a headache that they have; and/or they get excited about something because it looks so amazing and the sales conversation was so intriguing that they feel like if they could just add this one piece to their business, it would change everything (think pewter bullet).

And that is normally the beginning spot for the implementation of automation software.

However, sometimes it's not even that good.

The starting point is selected by a well meaning Infusionsoft employee or Infusionsoft Certified Consultant (ICC) with a checklist in front of them.

The business owner is so excited or overwhelmed that they have a list of 20 places to start, or they're not sure where to start so they turn over the decision making process to an individual with no clue about the nature of their business and it's core limitation.

It's hardly fair to the well meaning employee, the ICC or the business owner. None of them have any context or method for determining what the core limitation is, so they are left with a crap shoot.

Fortunately, not all is lost. Unfortunately, not all is lost.

What do I mean by fortunately?

One of the great things about good automation software is that there's probably some portion of it that would directly apply to the limitation of the business. And if they do something, there is a chance they could accidentally hit the core limitation and see tremendous profit growth. At this point the business owner is hooked on automation software and almost nothing can shake them!

This is a good thing, because it produced more profit, but it's also VERY UNFORTUNATE!

Why? Because now the business owner, the well meaning employee or ICC have created an association. Implement this automation technology and it will produce profit!

So they begin to indiscriminately apply the technology all over the business, almost with abandon. They may mistake residual effects of their accidental hit on the core limitation as outcomes from their undirected application of automation technology.

They continue to put automation to work at random, based on their whims, but then they hit the wall. Profit has plateaued and there is no explanation.

The business owner is left to wonder, *"Is this all I can do? Isn't there a way to grow profits further?"*

You can identify if you are on this road by simply answering one question: How much of Infusionsoft do you want to implement in your business?

Another way of finding out your answer is to ask yourself how would you respond too the question of "*Are you only using X % of Infusionsoft?*"

If you answered the first question with "*I want to use as much of Infusionsoft as possible!*" Or if you felt like you should be using more of Infusionsoft when you were asked if you are only using a portion of Infusionsoft, then you can safely determine you are on the wrong path to profits.

The entire notion that you need to, or ought to be trying to use any percentage of Infusionsoft with the emphasis toward using more is at odds with our basis for how profit flow is increased.

The focus is on the possible part of the sentence as opposed to the absolute part of the sentence.

If I've been describing where you've been, you can skip to the next chapter, because I need to speak quickly with...

The Stalled Business Owner

This is the more common scenario...

The business owner is overwhelmed by all the options and all the holes they see in their business and can't decide where to start.

I can immediately tell you when I'm talking to the stalled business owner. They always start out with the same line:

"*I may have been a little premature in getting Infusionsoft...*"

The truth is they were wise to invest in the technology. 99% of small business will benefit wildly from putting the correct part of automation software into place.

But if the stalled business owner isn't assisted quickly, their situation turns bad fast!

The Danger...

The reality is, unless they happen to stumble upon the one thing that is limiting profit in the business, they won't get the results they are after and then they become frustrated. And the natural inclination is, then, to blame the technology.

"*The technology must not work. This was a bunch of hogwash. They sold me a pipe dream.*"

This to me is the worst case scenario because it may cause the business owner to reject automation software entirely, or to seek another provider. Going to another provider won't fix the direction and the end result is outright frustration and an intolerance for automation technology which will ultimately be the downfall of the business.

Regardless if you have some immediate success and then focus on letting the technology lead your strategy or if you hesitate and then become frustrated with it, you are on the wrong path when you let technology lead out.

Chapter 6

THE RIGHT APPROACH TO AUTOMATION

If the wrong approach is to have technology or the percentage of the technology that is applied driving our decision making process, then what is the right approach?

Technology can produce profit if, and only if, the technology reduces the limitation on the flow of profit.

You'll recall that there is only one definite part of this short sentence.

It is the part that focuses in on the core limitation on the flow of profit. It logically follows that if we want to clarity of direction and a good deal of certainty when we act, then we need to feel confident that we are addressing the core limitation.

If your approach to adding automation software to your business starts by identifying what is truly limiting profit flow, then you are pointed in the right direction.

How Do You Determine The Core Limitation?

The first step to identifying what limits the flow of profit in your business is to break your business up into the most basic series of interdependent processes.

For most businesses, this will fall into something like:

- Lead generation,
- Lead conversion or Sales
- Fulfillment – the doing of the thing that creates the value that the customer is after.
- Billing – the collecting of the revenue generated by sales. This also covers pricing.
- These are the four basic pipes I've seen in almost every business I've come across. It may be the same for you.

At this stage I find it interesting to take a gut check and write down which pipe you think is limiting profit. In fact, to make it real interesting, let's do a quick survey.

Text LIMIT to (760) 621-8199...you can scan the QR Code if you prefer.

When you text the word LIMIT in my system will ask you to share your gut instinct on which pipe is limiting the flow of profit for you.

If you fully participate it will ask you tomorrow if you feel the same way. I'll send you a link to check out the survey results so you can see how you fit in!

The next step is to take those pipes and measure them.

Here are some starter questions to help you:

How many leads did the business generate in the last month?

What is the percentage of sales that closed last month relative to number of leads generated last month?

What is the percentage of work completed last month relative to sales reported in the last month?

What is the percentage of revenue collected last month relative to the work completed in the last month?

Maybe those measurements won't give a good picture of what is happening in your business, maybe they will. I'll let you determine how to adjust them to give an accurate picture, but the objective is to determine what the diameter of your pipes are right now.

Once you have these measurements for your business, you need to look at the business and be able to say, *"What is the relationship between two adjoining processes?"*

Let's look at an example; if we had 100 leads generated in a month and we had 10 sales, then we would say we had a 10 percent conversion.

10 percent of all the leads generated are represented as sales in that same month. That tells us a relationship between the two.

Then, we would go on to the next step. Let's say that we collect money as soon as the sale's made. What percentage of the sales made ended up in money collected?

If it's 100 percent, then we would know the relationship between the two and so on down the chain.

If we look at the pipe or the business in this fashion, then we can see a place at which there is a limitation.

If the limitation is in our ability to get leads, then what we'll notice is that we have a pretty close to 100 percent relationship between each adjoining pipe, meaning that what's controlling the flow of profit is the number of leads generated.

Once you've looked at your business in this fashion, you can determine what is actually limiting the flow of profit.

The following pages include examples of possible "*pipe*" configurations and what the numbers will show. Read through each example to get a feel for how your numbers may be expressed.

The Limitation: Lead Generation

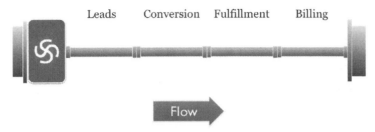

If your pipes all seem to be the same size, meaning you convert 100% of your leads to sales, fulfill on your marketing and sales promises perfectly and collect 100% of the revenue generated by sales, then leads limit the flow of profit!

If leads control your profit, beware! Until you begin to ramp up leads you have no idea how well you can really convert, fulfill and collect! The good news is generating leads is perhaps the easiest thing to do.

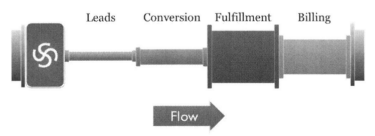

Although your current numbers tell you that your pipe is uniform in capacity, the truth may look something like this. In this scenario, once you improve lead flow, which pipe will you need to focus on next?

The Limitation: Lead Conversion

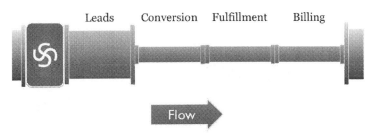

Leads   Conversion   Fulfillment   Billing

Flow

When asked which pipe configuration is ideal, I vote for this layout. However, I'd like there to be a higher conversion ratio than shown in this configuration.

Once you get to this configuration you want to focus on improving the quality of your leads, but you don't want to ramp up the number of leads.

A bulk of your focus must stay on improving the conversion process. Any time spent anywhere else will not increase profit significantly.

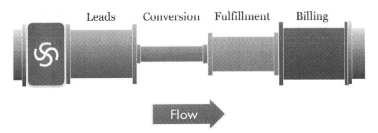

Leads   Conversion   Fulfillment   Billing

Flow

Again, while it may appear that our ability to fulfill and bill are not limited at all, which pipe will need attention once conversion as a limitation has be removed?

The Limitation: Fulfillment

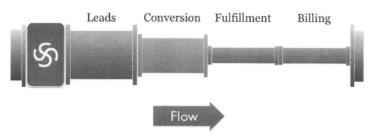

This configuration is bad news! When your ability to fulfill is the limitation you need to move FAST! Your reputation is in serious jeopardy because you're selling but not fulfilling on the promises made in sales and marketing.

Part of owning a growing business will at some point include having a business that sells faster than it can keep up. If this is your business don't feel like you've failed, but don't rest!

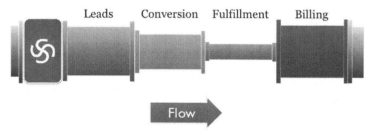

As you're probably noticing, just because the numbers say following pipes are at the same level, doesn't mean your capacity is at the same level. You'll only know it's current capacity when the limitation arrives at the pipe.

The Limitation: Billing

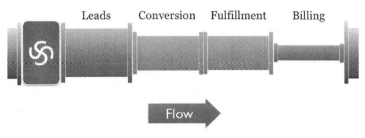

Leads   Conversion   Fulfillment   Billing

Flow

This is the worst position to have your business in, because you're putting out all the capital to generate lead, make sales, do what you promised and then not collect, or charge what you should!

No matter which configuration your business reveals it's helpful for a couple reasons. First, and foremost, it gives you a clear idea of where to start looking for the core limitation. Second it warns you of what impact the current limitation may be having on your business.

Your Reputation

If leads control the flow of profit in your business right now, it may not impact your reputation in the marketplace much at all...but that's only because you're a non-entity in the marketplace!

If your business is new, bad news, if you don't start ramping up leads fast you're in trouble!

You could have quite a bit of business. You could have tapped the entire market, in which case you've hit a wall. If that's the case you may determine that your limitation is the marketplace it's self.

The only possible solution may be to extend what your business does to open new markets.

If lead conversion is limiting your business, you could be causing your leads to believe that you don't need their business. If you're not adequately following up or addressing requests for more information, or simply not asking for the sale, your reputation is negatively impacted.

Can you see why just throwing more leads isn't the solution?

What if your limitation is your ability to meet the promises made in marketing and sales?

Does that negatively impact your reputation in the marketplace? Oh boy! You know it does!

"Have you done business with XYZ Corp?"

"Yes, and don't bother. Their sales pitch is great, but they couldn't get the job done!"

What's really bad when your ability to fulfill is your limitation is that you probably are not doing a great job for some and not doing a so well with others.

Across the board all of your customers are getting a lack luster performance from your company.

When I've found myself in this situation I would gradually pull back on lead generation as I ramped up the company's ability to fulfill and once I was confident I had removed the limitation I open up lead generation again until the next limitation reveals itself.

Finally, when collection is your limitation it means one of two things.One, you don't collect what's due. The marketplace loves this, but it's not good for you.

"Oh XYZ Corp, they are amazing! They really deliver! And to top it off, they take forever to get paid!"

There's only one thing worse than that.

Being pegged as the low price leader. If you don't charge enough, you could get the reputation of a price fighter. The lowest on the price chart. I don't know anyone who wants to play that game, at least not in reality.

The Perpetual Money Machine

Once you see which pipe is limiting profit, we have to get to the core limitation, in order to understand the nature of that limitation.

Let me give you an example.

As part of our training company, we offered a done for you marketing service. As part of this service, we produced marketing, we picked lists and we mailed out to prospects on behalf of our customers.

We called the program the Perpetual Money Machine.

We generated 50 to 100 phone calls each month for each of our customers.

Prior to working with us, our customers were generating anywhere from three to four leads per month.

Of those leads, they converted 100 percent to customers. They were able to fulfill on 100 percent. And they were able to collect on 100 percent.

As far as they were concerned if we generated a lead for them, they could close it, work it and get paid...no problem.

Their funnel looked like this:

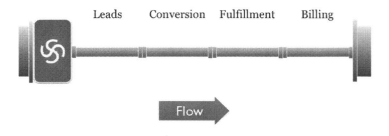

Well, when we turned on the lead flow for them and bumped them up to the 50 or 100 leads per month range, suddenly things changed! A series of pipes that looked like they were just straight and perfectly ready and capable of handling a lot more business ended up turning into something that wasn't as good as we hoped.

Their funnel changed to this:

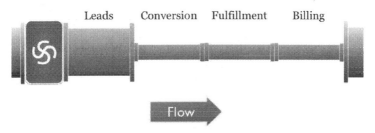

The ability for them to convert was in the four to six percent range. What had once been 100 percent suddenly looked like four to six percent because if they received 100 leads, they were only able to convert about 6 of those 100 leads into new customers.

What went wrong?

What was the limitation?

Obviously, the limitation was their ability to convert leads into sales. But why?

Initially, their first inclination was to **blame the quality of the leads**. But we knew that something was up, something deeper than just the quality of the leads. How did we know? Simply because our in house business that was receiving these same leads, was able to convert at a much higher rate.

We knew that it wasn't the quality of the leads.

We recognized that we needed to look at what was going on with their lead conversion process.

If this was the limitation, if conversion was the thing that was limiting the flow of profit, we needed to understand the nature of what was limiting the conversions so we could identify what technology would facilitate breaking or reducing that limitation.

We had a planned mastermind with these customers scheduled so I determined I would get the answer to the question that would reveal the nature of the limitation.

During a mastermind, I asked one pivotal and important question...

"What is your process for handling a lead?"

The process for 20 of the 21 participants was, "*I called the individual back. If they're ready, I make them a customer; if they're not, I put their name on a piece of* paper or in a spreadsheet and intend to call them back later."

When pressed further, the 20 who had this same system confessed that they may not have called back all of the leads that were generated for them and, of those they called back that were not ready to do business, they had not followed up with any of them at all.

This gave me insight into the limitation.

The limitation was not their ability to sell.

The limitation that they had run into was the limitation of time.

They did not have enough time in the day for them to call and reach all of the prospects, to be able to follow up with them and take care of fulfillment and take care of collections.

In order for them to run the business, they had to spend time in all areas of the business and the time that they spent on lead conversion was insufficient to deal with the big influx of leads that we had created for them. Time was what was limiting them.

How do you reduce the limitation of time?

Far as I know, nobody can create more time, so how are we supposed to reduce this limitation when it seems as though it's a finite thing...a fixed thing that can't be changed?

We looked at the nature of why time was such a limitation. What was it that they wanted to do with each lead that was blocked by a lack of time.

When I asked what would be the ideal follow up process, they expressed that it would involve many more touches, potentially in multiple medias, not just a phone call, but also direct mail, email, maybe even a text message.

As a result, there was no way for them to do all these things with the limited amount of time they had. However, this answer revealed to us exactly what technology we needed to look for.

We needed to look for a technology that would allow everyone who called in to be sent some basic information that would begin the selection process to segregate the leads until they could talk with each lead.

Part of what kept them from calling every lead was the duration from when the call came in, to the time when they could call back. If had been more than two weeks, they felt like it had been too long to call.

Next, once they go the prospect on the phone, they would make some sort of determination of what the needs were of the prospect; and if the prospect decided not to do business at that point in time, why.

Then, they needed to be able to, in some sort of automated fashion, follow up with these individuals.

For you, if you're a customer of automation software, you would see an easy solution to their problem.

But, for these individuals, they were not aware of the technology.

They had accepted, at first, as fact that they couldn't get back to everybody as a fact of life. And this is really important.

Understand that these were very successful business owners. They were some of the top in their class because of the transaction size was a value of anywhere between $6,000.00 and $18,000.00.

They didn't have to do a whole lot of sales each month in order for them to hit their targets. Being able to convert three to four prospects per month was a good thing for most of their businesses.

Being able to do 8 or 10 would have been even better, but they were able to survive without this big influx of leads. How were they able to survive on three to four?

Well, there was enough money there. There was enough time for them to respond to three to four prospects without issue.

When we changed the dynamic of the business by creating an influx of 50 to 100 new leads, we also challenged the rules that had allowed them to survive as a business and we actually started to create some chaos in the business.

Obviously, this wasn't our intention, but this brings up a very important point about the right approach to automation software and that is to recognize that rules will have to change in conjunction with the technology.

Let's look at the solution we came up with for them and how that impacted their ability to be able to do business more effectively and increase profit.

The solution we came up with for them was a series of automated messages that would be delivered in email and direct mail as well as prompts for them to make a phone call at a pivotal point in the conversation.

Through the use of automation software, we were able to create these messages and have them be delivered in a timed sequence that would allow them to stay in touch with the prospect for a long time beyond the initial phone call.

Next we looked at the four most common concerns that the prospects raised that caused them decide not to do business.

We wrote campaigns or a series of messages delivered through email, direct mail and phone conversations and fashioned those so that, as our customer got off the phone with the prospect, they would be able to make a determination based on the conversation and add the prospect to the sequence.

If they didn't get a hold of the prospect they would apply a campaign of emails and direct mail and phone calls to that prospect.

In the past, their rule had been call them once. If they don't convert, put them on a list, but don't go back to the list or do anything with that list.

Had they maintained that rule of just marking them as sold or not in the software and moving on, we wouldn't have changed their results.

The profit flow would not have increased.

We changed the rule to leverage the technology that reduced the limitation of time.

The NEW rules: If we don't get a hold of them on the phone, add them to this other campaign. And, if they do fall into one of the four camps, add them to that campaign. If we do sell them, then go ahead and move them into the customer category.

If they had not followed these new rules, it wouldn't have mattered how fantastic the technology was. And I have to tell you that some of the people didn't follow the new rules.

Some of the people continued with the same operation, the same processes that they had before.

They would make the call and, instead of remembering to drop them into the automated campaign, they would do nothing. And, as a result, they saw no change in their ability to convert leads.

However, those that did change the rules did see the increase in their ability to convert leads and, as a result, their profits.

Now, if you followed the process up until this point and stopped short of identifying old rules that allowed you to survive without the technology and failed to identify and formalize the new rules that would leverage the technology that reduces the limitation, you wouldn't see a change in profit flow.

You may incorrectly assume that I was full of malarky. How sad would that be?

Unfortunately those who stumble upon the limitation in their business by some other method are generally unaware of the importance of changing the rules.

I can not over state this, or over emphasize this, or over state this. As you investigate the core limitation, and seek to understand the nature of it, you must identify how the company has managed to survive in spite of it!

Looking back at our example, what would have happened to my customers' businesses had they dropped everything else they were doing and only called back leads, wrote cards to the leads, and sent emails.

Would they have converted more? Probably, but at what cost? Their ability to fulfill? Their ability to collect? Keeping the business afloat demanded that they pick a less than optimal rule for dealing with leads, but it was the best thing they could have done to keep the business going!

The rule they followed was a great rule given the limitation that existed in the business. It's extremely important that you believe this. The rules that allow you to survive in spite of the core limitation are great rules...while the limitation is there.

It's only once you've identified what technology needs to be put in place to reduce the limitation that the rules need to be replaced.

The new rules must be formalized. I use a replacement language when establishing rules with private clients after implementing a new technology based solution that addresses the core limitation.

I'll say something like this:

> *Before we added these 6 new automated follow up sequences you would call once and then mark the prospect for a future call if they didn't covert.*
>
> *Now you'll add all prospects to the initial follow up sequence and then begin calling them back. If you are able to reach them and they don't convert, you'll seek to determine which of the four concerns is dominant for them and tag them with the corresponding tag that will start the correct sequence.*
>
> *Each morning before you start your initial return calls you'll call back any prospects the sequences prompt you to call.*

Did you notice how we were able to find the technology?

I purposefully waited a few pages to bring this up. If you need to you can go back and review. In order to find the technology needed we first identified the ideal solution.

Notice that the solution was fully determined before technology was selected. Why is that so critical?

All along I've repeated the fact that what we really want is significant profit growth. I went so far as to challenge you to determine a multiple you'd like to grow profit this year. Did you notice that in my example I even suggested a 300% growth rate?

How in the world can you sustain that kind of growth? Is it even possible to do year after year?

I'll tell you this much...it is impossible to do when you nuder your plans to reduce a limitation by considering first what technology you have available and then create an implementation plan.

As soon as you are clear on the nature of the core limitation, don't you dare to begin to think about which technology would address it!

First map out the ideal solution to reduce or eliminate the core limitation. Although I've only made reference to automation software in relation to technology, the reality is that technology may be a process, hardware, software or even people with specific skill sets.

So before you pigeon hole yourself into using only a software to address the limitation, open yourself up to the possibility that anything could be part of the solution. The most powerful solutions may detail out technologies that you are unaware of.

I know that many of the features of Infusionsoft that we now employ we were unaware of as we mapped out an ideal solution.

Once we have an ideal solution, then we form a checklist of technologies we will need to employ to make that solution reality.

If you'll follow this process you'll find that your results are orders of magnitude greater than if you think *"What can I build with what I know about?"*

Get really clear on what it is that you want to do in an ideal world, then start searching for the technology that matches versus looking at what technology you have available and adapting your solution.

This is the number one way people reduce their ability to grow profit dramatically.

When you handicap your solution because you think about the things that you already know how to do versus exploring and finding those things that can do what you're ideal solution is, you reduce your ability to – you kill your ability to reduce the limitation and create that dynamic growth that we're really looking for.

OK, so you have the ideal plan and you even identified the technologies that will make it happen.

Is it time to begin investing? Before we begin to invest in the build out of the solution we do one last check. We work through how the technology will work and try and identify what might not work.

We identify what rules would need to be formalized to leverage the technology and then analyze if the people who will be interacting with the technology will be able to or inclined to follow the new rules.

Just because a habit will need to be changed with the new rules doesn't mean we won't move forward. But we do get prepared to explain the why behind the rule change.

Believe it or not, most employees want to do a good job (assuming you're not a total jerk). In fact, the very existence of the old rules prove it. What causes employee disfunction more often than not is they don't understand the why behind the rule.

As you are analyzing your solution you're trying to anticipate what why needs to be explained to go along with the new rules. You may be pleasantly surprised that when your staff understands the why they will enhance your rules even further to leverage the technology even more.

The other day a member of my staff was telling me about a recent research project where folks were pushing the envelope of how far self driving cars could go.

Before self driving cars can become a staple on the road, it would be good to see how far they could go, so they determined to see how well a computer could drive a car at 150 miles per hour.

As part of the study they also brought in human drivers as a control. They had mapped out the very best paths through the various courses for optimal race times and then tracked how close the humans were able to drive those same lines.

They were amazed to discover that humans had incredible precision and operated with computer like accuracy.

I was not surprised.

Humans have an amazing sense for the limits around them. With a little practice they can sense how far they can go at an unconscious level. It's quite amazing. When it comes to driving we can be so good we get in trouble.

People read, text, day dream and do many other activities as they drive on a crowded road with hundreds of other drivers who's actions they couldn't hope to predict in a million years.

Likewise, your sense for business is incredible. The fact that you can turn a profit while often relying on not much more than your gut feeling is amazing.

But what you'll be able to do as you refine your instincts by following the method I've laid out in this book will be inspiring.

A Solemn Warning...

The number one mistake that you can make in this whole process is to pick the wrong limitation; something that doesn't actually limit the flow of profit.

One of my core beliefs is that, as a business owner, you have gut instincts that will help you to identify core limitations.

There are things that are in your business that you just hate, some of which you may have accepted as facts of life.

If you're not sure about this limitation, one of the sure fire ways to determine it is actually the core limitation, is to bring someone in with fresh eyes that understands this process.

The reason being is because with fresh eyes, they can ask the stupid questions that we call stupid questions because it seems as though the answer is so obvious.

However, with a fresh set of eyes and understanding the process we've outlined here, looking at your business, they can see things that you have accepted as a fact of life; limitations that you have accepted as being just the way things are.

If we were to have talked to people 200 years ago about the ability to travel from San Diego to New York in a matter of hours, they would have thought we were insane because the facts of life were there was no way you could travel that distance in that short a period of time.

The technology simply wasn't available and the limitation was assumed to be just a fact of life. You'll never be able to travel that fast in that short a period of time.

However, with today's technology, we take it for a fact of life that you can travel that quickly.

There are things in your business, limitations that exist, that you have come to accept as a matter of necessity in order for your business to continue to exist.

And you have developed rules and processes to allow your business to exist in spite of the limitation.

Chapter 7

FOCUS ON PROFIT NOT TECHNOLOGY

One of the big challenges we have as business owners is being distracted by all of the messages that are coming at us.

One of the most common things I hear from my private clients is that they feel like they are constantly getting pulled in by sales pitches and as a result distracted.

They come to the conclusion that the only way to insulate themselves from distraction is to insulate themselves from outside messages.

While on the surface, this might seem like a good idea, this is a very bad idea because, as a business owner, you do need to be aware of new technology.

You need to be aware of those things that have the potential to reduce limitations.

But, what you need even more is to have a structure for dealing with all that information.

Because most of us weren't born with the structure, or method for handling all this information coming at us or a way of analyzing that information effectively so that we can determine if it should become a priority for our business or not, we end up being swayed by every wind of doctrine.

Everything that comes at us ends up pushing us in one direction or another.

Fortunately, there is a secret to being able to be exposed to a lot of different messages – sales messages, new technologies, etc, without it becoming a distraction to your business.

First, you need to be always focused on profit.

You need to make sure that when you do anything in your business, it's always because you've analyzed it for it's potential to create profit now.

Will this change affect profit in a positive way?

Will it **dramatically** increase profit growth?

If it's not going to dramatically increase profit growth, then it doesn't even get a second glance. How do we determine what is going increase profit growth?

By being aware of the core limitation in our business.

Being aware of where the limitation is now and where it appears to be shifting next and then using measurements, very simple measurements, like those I asked you to use to determine where the limitation is in your business right now, as a means of checking on where the business is in terms of potential and opportunity for growth.

Once we've done that and once we have that as part of our rituals in our business that each month we verify where the status is of the business in terms of what's the current limiting factor of the business and we continue to apply the solutions that are addressed in that core limitation.

At this point, when we have this process ingrained into us and into our business, now we're open to be exposed to all messages without them impacting us because every message that we receive, we now will classify under the pipes that make up your business.

And we just take each of the pipes, give them a name and this is now a category for all information that we're exposed to.

If we see some radical new technology that has to do with lead capture, then we don't worry about if we need to implement that right now or not because seeing it is not determining if we need to implement it.

Seeing it is just making us aware of it.

We take that information and we classify it.

In this case, we said it was a new technology that had to do with lead capture, so we would put that in the lead capture category.

If our business is telling us that the thing that's limited our ability to generate more profit is our ability to capture leads, then this becomes a priority.

We look at, *"What is the true nature of the limitation for our business?"*, and if the limitation for our business is our ability to capture, then we look and say, *"What is the nature of the limitation and how can we now use this information that's being presented to us to address the solution, the ideal solution we came up? Does it fulfill the needs of an item on our technology checklist that came out of our ideal solution that was created from our deep understanding of the current limitation on the business?"*

If it is, then, great. We go and we implement it; if it isn't, then we put it on the shelf in that category,.

Whether that's a mental shelf or a digital shelf or an actual physical shelf, we put that idea on the shelf and we leave it there until that becomes a priority.

You can be exposed to sales pitches of all kinds.

If someone is selling something and it's enticing and exciting, it's okay for us to feel those emotions because what we're going do now is we're going take that and we're going categorize it.

Does that fall into the sales conversion?

Does that fall into the fulfillment?

And we'll go ahead and mark that and then, we ask ourselves, *"Is this the one thing that's limiting profit?"*

And the decision isn't made by the emotion. The decision isn't made by our excitement about this new technology or this new idea or this new concept.

But, our decisions are made based on what the business is telling us will generate greater profit growth.

And if the thing we're hearing or being exposed to isn't directly related to that thing that limits profit growth, then we categorize it and we put it on the shelf for when our business tells us it's ready for it.

This is a revolutionary way of looking at the information that you'll be exposed to as a business owner and it allows you to operate freely in an environment where all sorts of message are being put out.

But, if you keep your focus on profit and not on technology, not on the latest fad, not on the newest thing, then you also insulate yourself from something that's called Bright, Shiny Object Syndrome.

This is a syndrome that has reached epidemic proportions and is sweeping the world. Because as people get interested in new technology, they find that that technology drives the decisions that they make in their business and this is exactly the wrong thing to do and you now know that.

Putting it to Work

If you haven't already text VIDEO to (760) 621-8199 to receive 4 videos from a presentation I gave on how to find out what your pipes are and how to discover your limitation. When you text in you'll receive a link to the videos. (You can scan the QR Code below to pull up the SMS ready to send)

I gave this presentation in September 2012 to a small group of hand picked individuals in San Diego. I was told later by one of them that they stayed in the parking lot talking about what I had taught them for well over an hour. They said it was more valuable to them than any $3,000 training they had ever attended.

You can be the judge...

Chapter 8

THE BUSINESS OWNER'S ROLE

Your role as the business owner is a very unique role and it's a very important role because, if you don't do your job correctly, if you don't fulfill your role in the business properly, the result is a business that fails.

That's a lot of pressure to put on one person, but it's the pressure that you've elected to take as being one of the elite group that we call entrepreneurs.

As an elite member of the entrepreneur class, it is your responsibility to take on the proper role.

Recently, I went on a cruise and that cruise went to the destinations that were scheduled at the time scheduled and arrived back at our port in the time that it was scheduled to go.

The captain of that ship, was successful in fulfilling his or her role.

Another boat that was out at sea at the same time as ours was not successful and, for whatever reason, the captain of that boat was not able to get that boat to the port on time.

In fact, it was delayed a full day.

You can imagine, if you're on a small cruise, three, four days, and your boat comes in a day late? What is the impact?

What is the impact on all the people that were on that boat in terms of, maybe, they had business that they needed to attend to?

Maybe they had family that they needed to attend to. What was the impact of that captain being a day late?

It was tremendous.

As the captain of your ship, you cannot afford to be a day late. You have to be on time. And the only way you can be on time is if you actually focus on your role.

Do you think that if the captain was busy in the engine room, working in the engine room or busy in the kitchen, working in the kitchen, that he could focus on the job that he had at hand?

And the answer is no. His responsibility was too great to allow him to be distracted by anything that wasn't the highest and best use of his time.

And the same is true for you.

You have a job as master strategist.

Your job is to make sure that the business is headed in the right direction; that the marketing and sales are happening as they should; that they're correctly reflecting what it is your business does; that your business does what it says it will do in the marketing and sales properly; that you're identifying opportunities that are up and coming and you're able to take advantage of them; but, not be distracted by opportunities that will lessen your business' ability to generate a profit.

All this comes together for you as the owner of the business and your role as master strategist.

One of the common mistakes that I see master strategist make is they try and learn automation software.

Learning the capabilities of automation software falls within the role of the business owner.

Implementing automation software does **not**.

If you have determined, because of the size of your business, that you are the one that has to implement automation software, I am truly and deeply sorry.

This means that your time can be worth no more than $20.00 an hour.

I understand that, over time, this number may change, but at the time of the writing of this book, if your time is worth anything over $20.00 an hour, then you have no business implementing automation software.

Why do I say that? Because any person that's working for $10.00 to $20.00 an hour can be taught to master building out processes in automation software.

In contrast, the time and effort that is going go into learning automation software can't be yours.

Quite frankly, your business cannot afford to invest your time, and your effort and your focus on learning any software of this nature, even if the automation software claims that it has been designed and developed for small business owners to use it.

The fact of the matter is, if you have a limited, finite number of hours of each day that can be devoted to your labors as a business owner.

And if any of those hours are spent or invested on things that are not your highest and best use of time, I can make a prediction, a very solid prediction about how your business is going to turn out and it's not pretty.

As you spend more time doing the things that you know that you should be doing as a business owner and less time doing the things you know you should not be doing as a business owner, you are going to see the results that you're after.

In fact, that leads me to a final discussion on the two most important measures that you as a business owner can have.

The first one is...

What did you do today, that you should not have done?

How many things did you do today that you should not have done? The higher the number the less effective you were. Sure you were busy, sure you worked hard, but you were not effective if you spent time on things you should not have been doing.

What did you not do today, that you should have?

How many? What were the critical few things that you should have accomplished, but you did not? This is a measure of your reliability. If you had shareholders, would they feel like they can rely on you to do what you should?

These two measures are the measures that can keep you on track. At the end of each day, if you can answer those two questions honestly, they will tell you how well you're fulfilling your role as the owner of the business.

Be honest with yourself on these two questions.

Be clear about what it is that you are the very best at, that only you must do and that cannot be done by anybody else.

Are you the one that's strategizing and creating the ideas for things to be implemented in automation software based on the process we covered in this book?

If you are, then you're doing the right thing.

If you're the one actually trying to implement the plan in the software, you're doing the wrong thing.

Make sure that you do the right things and avoid the wrong things.

Measure yourself in terms of those two questions:

- *"What things did you do today that you should not have been doing?"* and
- *"What things did you not do today that you should have been doing?"*

Use those two questions to propel yourself to focus in on the right things and, as you do it with the method you've learned in this book, I guarantee you will see more profit generated out of your business.

-Ryan J Chapman